MW00562664

PORCH LIVING

PORCH LIVING

JAMES T. FARMER III

PHOTOGRAPHS BY HELEN NORMAN

GIBBS SMITH
TO ENRICH AND INSPIRE HUMANKIND

To Mimi and Granddaddy—your families taught you to
live graciously, as you have me. Thank you. —JTFIII

To my family, I am so grateful for all the wonderful times we
have shared on our porch, the favorite place to gather. —HN

First Edition
16 15 14 13 12   5 4 3 2 1

Text © 2012 by James T. Farmer III
Photographs © 2012 by Helen Norman

All rights reserved. No part of this book may be reproduced by any
means whatsoever without written permission from the publisher,
except brief portions quoted for purpose of review.

Published by
Gibbs Smith
P.O. Box 667
Layton, Utah 84041

1.800.835.4993 orders
www.gibbs-smith.com

Designed by Drew Furlong
Printed and bound in Hong Kong

Gibbs Smith books are printed on paper produced from sustain-
able PEFC-certified forest/controlled wood source. Learn more
at www.pefc.org.

ISBN 978-1-4236-2534-6
Library of Congress Control Number: 2011943941

CONTENTS

INTRODUCTION

Stemming literally from words of antiquity, the *porch* has been our greeting and gathering place for centuries. Grandiose and humble, classic and modern, country and city, these vestibules of nostalgia and welcome are our homes' first and last impressions. The porch is an architectural welcome mat, a social scene, and a hybrid of home and garden.

It is this combination of home and garden that makes porch living ever so delightful! *En plein air* melding with the great indoors forms a perfect union that both venues afford—this is the essence of a porch.

Pots of geraniums, urns of ferns, tables laden with treats, and pitchers full of lemonade and glistening with condensation—food and flowers—nature's best and all a part of the porch's tableau. Rockers and swings cushioned with pillows, chairs weathered and worn from years of good use, and lanterns extending the light just a bit longer invite us to linger a while or beckon us home. These are the characters on the porch stage—a scene worth embracing and enjoying.

So sit back, relax, swing, rock, or simply perch yourself on the porch. Greet your neighbors and the sunrise or sunset. Enjoy this part of your home and set a new standard of living for your friends and yourself.

CLASSIC COUNTRY & RUSTIC PORCHES

A country porch, whether fine or rustic, is as comforting and familiar as a glass of tea on a warm summer's day. The porch may be a relaxing retreat to unwind from the day or even brace the dawn.

LEFT A truly classic country porch with rustic flair for this mountain setting. Wood, stone and foliage aplenty set the tone for this lovely locale.

9

LEFT As vestibule between home and outdoors, the porch is a fine spot to towel off from a quick dip, an afternoon shower, or a soggy garden saunter.

RIGHT Keeping in tone with the architecture, even the tableware nods in homage to the setting. A woodland scene is perfectly apropos for this porch tableau.

Classic Country & Rustic Porches

Classic Country & Rustic Porches

LEFT Leashes, totes and wide-brim hats—porch accoutrements are at hand, ready and waiting for an afternoon walk or a jaunt into the garden.

RIGHT Welcome home! Pots brimming with foliage and flowers welcome you and yours to the porch—a perfect example of the porch as your home's first and last impression.

LEFT Whether it holds a collection of folk art or is a spot to catch up on your reading list, a screened stage is set to suit your fancy.

ABOVE Porch living at its finest! With a garden coup nearby, you never know who will try to sit and sip a glass of lemonade with you on your porch!

Whether it's a place to plop and drop,
rest and relax, or just catch a glance at
the view—whatever your favorite
porch perch is, savor each moment.

LEFT Indoor/outdoor fabrics pair with garden collections on this porch. The color of the begonia harmonizes with the pillow and cushion combo and graces the whole scene, complete with antique trowels and a stack of magazines awaiting perusal.

ABOVE LEFT A vintage pillow depicts a coastal scene. What better place to tell this pillow's story than a porch?

ABOVE RIGHT A trilogy of topiaries. The porch can be a garden extension too, showcasing a favorite plant collection.

19

Dappled shade from centurion sentries
and ever-so-slight peeks of blue sky pierce the
canopy of trees. A lush lace of azaleas skirts
the porch, too, thus a mantle of classicism and
nostalgia envelope the home.

ABOVE Live oaks whisper through Spanish moss as the ferns dance in the Lowcountry breeze. A quintessential Southern welcoming place, the porch gives its guests a spot to alight after travel and embrace the setting.

RIGHT Tradition with a twist. A perfectly classic country porch comes to life with a delightful blend of old and new, vintage and modern.

Classic Country & Rustic Porches

LEFT The porch becomes a gardener's potager and a tableau.

ABOVE LEFT The color of robins' eggs and electricity combined, this swing sparks from the deep, shady recesses of the porch.

ABOVE RIGHT The porch, its steps, niches and nooks are the perfect spots to show off garden heirlooms and accents.

Classic Country & Rustic Porches

What once was old is new again. Porches are donned with our personalities, delights and pizzazz! These venues are our guests' first glimpse into our home and style.

FAR LEFT A trio of vintage metal cases become fern stands and caladium caches on this porch. Old wood and new mirrored glass reflect the bucolic scene.

LEFT Finds from nature and the past. Even a cool porch can afford a chic and stylish breeze from a vintage fan.

RIGHT Kick off your boots—keep the garden mud in the garden! Then sit and relax and enjoy your handiwork from your porch.

A view toward
the home from
the porch, where
shutters and
flowers accent
the architecture.
The porch is a
hybrid of garden
and home.

Classic Country & Rustic Porches

RIGHT A window box billowing with summer's grandeur
looks ever so sharp with a soft blue provincial shutter
seemingly expanding the width of the window.

As faithful as a canine companion, the porch will always stand true as a destination of solace, tranquility and, of course, the best lemonade stand around.

LEFT The lushness of magnolia and the cacophony of greens from the garden inspired the deep green color of the rockers and swing.

RIGHT Ready and waiting—a table nestled on a corner of the porch invites folks to partake in the delights of the season.

"Come sit a spell or just chat." "Come calling on our porch and let's catch up." These are the notes beckoning neighbors and friends to spend time together on the porch.

Classic Country & Rustic Porches

LEFT A coastal Georgia porch in true Southern "double porch" style is doubly comfortable and welcoming. Long-leaf pine and live oak add shade to the garden, viewable from the porches aloft.

Extensions of our
homes, porches
prove themselves
as outdoor
venues perfect
for entertaining,
visiting or simply
playing with a
new kitten.

RIGHT Dark shutters and rockers contrast with the pale
yellow exterior. A precious little girl plays with her new kitten under the shade of her family's porch. Some things are
just classic!

Palm fronds sway and rustle, rhythmic lullabies for a porch swing. Ocean air, garden scents and notes of children laughing waft onto this porch to further relax our minds and spirits and prepare for porch living as it may be best—porch resting!

Classic Country & Rustic Porches

LEFT Nesting on this fantastic swing is porch living at its finest. Swaying palm fronds lull you to sleep ever so gently.

CASUALLY ELEGANT PORCHES

A juxtaposition of indoors and outdoors, casual and elegant, the porch is an extension of the home and garden proper. From the welcome of shade to the graciousness of comfortable seating, the casually elegant porch is the spot for such enjoyment.

LEFT A compilation of wicker and rattan makes for lovely seating and accents on this casually elegant porch.

Casually Elegant Porches

LEFT Worn bakery implements and wooden fragments accent a wall. Touches of green make the scene come alive.

ABOVE Stripes on stripes. A striking combo of fabrics adds comfortable elegance to this porch's aesthetic value.

Casually Elegant Porches

Whether screened,
opened or glassed,
the porch is a
part of the home's
architecture.
Elements farther
from the
porch become
points in the
architectural view.

RIGHT An elegantly ornate wrought-iron gate leads from the porch to an expansive lawn.

Casually Elegant Porches

ABOVE LEFT Fine screening keeps the bugs at bay but does not obstruct the fabulous marsh view on this coastal Georgia porch.

ABOVE RIGHT The gathering place—a niche within a niche—this porch's fireplace has hosted many an evening chat and even a s'more or two.

RIGHT Fitting perfectly within the stately architecture of this screened window, a porch swing sets the tone for relaxed living.

Its arms opened wide, the porch beckons
visitors through open doors, inviting
them to linger a bit longer.

LEFT A classic combo of wood and wicker is perfectly
at home on this porch. The faint blue-green ceiling
echoes the natural world beyond the screen.

ABOVE Bifold doors double the width of the home's
opening, graciously and grandly embracing porch living.

With vistas
abounding, a
porch's ledge may
just be the roost to
command a view.

Casually Elegant Porches

LEFT Tone-on-tone cushions and wicker soften the stone-work structural elements of this porch. Soft sheers are an unusual and fully effective choice for making a shady, private retreat.

Casually Elegant Porches

The beauty of complements— stone and flowers— along with a side table of hard materials and a lamp that wears both hardware and a soft shade, wraps up the idea of elegant living that the porch embodies.

RIGHT Garden flowers, repurposed tables and swaths of fabric bring the comforts of inside to this outside venue.

Details in nature are emulated in design, and what better place for this emulation than the porch. From the hosting of parties to that quiet moment before the day begins, we relish the details a well-appointed porch can afford.

LEFT This chic cottage porch is filled with lush vases of semi-tropical foliage, a classic fabric and plenty of light sources to enjoy the porch longer once the sun has set.

ABOVE LEFT A large clamshell serves double duty as fruit "basket" and porch accessory.

ABOVE RIGHT Layer upon layer, tone upon tone: the versatility of outdoor fabrics makes the porch as fashionable as any room in the house.

Casually Elegant Porches

LEFT A series of arches frames the view into the garden, while fine-mesh screening gives the garden and porch a symbiotic nod.

RIGHT Collections of garden goodness are gathered and displayed casually and elegantly on this gorgeous stone porch.

Casually Elegant Porches

ABOVE LEFT A literal extension of the home, this porch elongates the living space of the home directly into the garden.

ABOVE RIGHT Details such as screening and doors reveal the connection between porch and home, or garden and home.

RIGHT Atop a landing, a settee provides this perfect spot to watch the children play or reflect upon the day.

The neutrality of green—the color is swathed throughout nature and is completely apropos for a porch. Though separated from the outdoors by only a screen, the green walls allow nature and architecture to blend harmoniously.

Casually Elegant Porches

LEFT A splash of tropical whimsy and white wicker casually meld together to form a truly elegant porch setting.

Casually Elegant Porches

LEFT A sun porch serves as galley and gallery, connecting the original home to a flawless addition. Garden, too, serves as vehicle between architectural points.

RIGHT Through the garden gate, a trail of cobbles and a roundabout around sedums lead to a warm glassed porch and entry.

Casually Elegant Porches

ABOVE Details such as faux bois pottery, silvery gray-green walls and a branch of red bud foliage create a vignette on this porch.

RIGHT Simultaneously an entry, a potting shed and a place to relax, this porch embodies the best blend of home and garden.

It may simply be a door, but the magic of opening it and being transported into a fusion of spaces is truly enchanting. The vestibule formed by the amalgamation of house and landscape boasts elements of both.

Casually Elegant Porches

LEFT A unique mantel with interesting carvings makes for a terrific focal point on this porch.

Casually Elegant Porches

Shady places
to greet neighbors
and retreat from
a rainstorm,
porches have
now claimed their
place as prime
outdoor living and
gardening spaces.

RIGHT Set, primed and ready for company! Once the garden party moves toward the home, this porch will be filled with laughter and fun rapport. The bubbly conversations will flow onto the porch, extending the life of the party started in the garden.

Casually Elegant Porches

LEFT The marriage of styles proves most successful on this European-style porch set in a Deep South garden. Like the abundant garden beyond, this porch mimics the home's architecture and approach to gracious living.

RIGHT Casting light once nature's source has set, lanterns allow us to read into the evening on our cool summer porches.

SLEEPING & LAZING PORCHES

Sleeping porches are steeped in nostalgia. Whether an escape from heat or a chance for soothing rest, bed yourself on the porch and dream of your garden and your home, for here one is amidst the two.

LEFT A full-sized bed awaits its guest on this sleeping porch. Dappled sunlight through the vines warms the sleeper and casts perfect naptime light.

Sleeping & Lazing Porches

ABOVE From daylight to dusk, a porch ledge rimmed with candles will extend one's rest time. A soothing scene of green and white aids relaxation.

RIGHT Couch, sofa, settee or bench—find your preference and anchor your porch with one. Lazing about the afternoon here is all too enticing.

When the season and weather perform as a perfect pair, living on the porch is at its utmost enjoyment. From sitting to sleeping, a porch can provide the locale.

LEFT Pillows, blankets and throws abound, creating a niche for napping on this sleeping porch. An old hayrack has been repurposed as storage for those additional covers.

ABOVE A scene of a sleeping porch in its entirety: from sofa to bed, niches to nest and nap abound.

Sleeping & Lazing Porches

Perhaps your porch
bids a bed-swing
shaded by beams,
shielding from the
afternoon sun; or
maybe a chaise padded
just right for napping;
or some comfy
chairs prompting a
long conversation.
Whatever the offer,
reading, relaxing and
laughing, too, are ideal
on a lazing porch.

RIGHT An intimate corner prompts a long, luxurious
sit with a friend.

Balance, scale and thus harmonious design aid our attempts to relax and enjoy these seemingly rare moments. The porch venue is no exception for this dictum of design.

Sleeping & Lazing Porches

LEFT When morning breaks our nocturnal slumber, extend the time with tea or coffee on the porch. A morning porch is perfect for such extension.

Sleeping & Lazing Porches

Swinging beds and porch swings may morph into the same, for sleeping and lazily lulling on the porch are a well-suited duo. With a view offering grand aesthetic value, shutting one's eyes might be difficult.

LEFT Pattern and tonal blends make for high design. The navy-and-white scheme is fitting for this coastal porch.

RIGHT Strong chain lines suspend this porch swing and direct the viewer toward the marsh. A range of pillow shapes and sizes plus a throw help nestle in the nap-taker towards the view.

Sleeping & Lazing Porches

Lazing about with garden views and garden-themed accessories is double delight. Fabulous prints and fabrics create attractive and pleasant recesses.

RIGHT A calico of collected objets d'art are fabulously appealing to all the senses on this well-groomed coastal cottage porch.

Sleeping & Lazing Porches

Luxurious lolling
under the shade
of pavilions and
porches—the finest
moments life may
afford. With pools
and recreation just
beyond, a spot for
rest also aids in the
constant complement
of indoor and outdoor
zeal that is a porch.

RIGHT Balancing act. A pair of outdoor sofa lounges
face one another and offer their guests rest from a dip
in the pool.

When covers, trellises, roofs and awnings are not present, an open terrace is simply an extension of the covered porch. Perfecting the harmony of indoors within an outdoor setting, the terrace may offer the porch's same comforts.

Sleeping & Lazing Porches

LEFT Chaises lined and ready. Lounge chairs padded for comfort are stylishly arranged alongside the pool.

Sleeping & Lazing Porches

Original concepts of porches derived from overhangs in nature, providing shelter from the elements. Still today, overhangs provide shelter from the elements, though the elements possibly aren't as threatening and the overhangs are much more stylish.

RIGHT anchoring the porch and pool pavilion, a stone fireplace links the two spaces. The covered porch is vestibule to the home from the garden, pool and landscape.

Enhancing the
essences nature
provides—ceiling
fans for additional
breeze and fireplaces
for added warmth.
The outdoor pavilion
or covered porch,
surrounded by a
cloak of greenery,
evokes that
magical sense of
balance between
home and garden.

Sleeping & Lazing Porches

LEFT Bluestone and fieldstone are softened with uphol-
stered, cushioned seating in this garden-set porch. Planters
bring added traces of the garden and seasonal accents too.

For after-school lessons or just reading for fun, a porch swing invites us to broaden the depths of our knowledge, search for the zenith of our imaginations, or simply calls us into peaceful snoozes for a luxurious afternoon nap.

RIGHT Laughter and glee arise from a funny line in the book or maybe even a joke between siblings. These two children find lazing fun while the family dog finds time for some quick shut-eye on this swinging bed under the deck.

PORCHES FOR ENTERTAINING

The porch is our home's most multifaceted room. Dining—from finest of fine to the most casual—is exceptional on the porch. It is this indoor/outdoor entertaining space that garners the best of both realms and shapes our lives into series of memorable moments.

LEFT A square glass-top table sets a contemporary vibe on this rustic porch. The traditional dinnerware gives a nod to the past, while the banquettes and chairs provide texture and visual appeal.

Porches for Entertaining

LEFT A sun porch flooded with light allows this homeowner to dine within the lushness of a garden even when winter has set in.

RIGHT Collections of collections. This niche on the sun porch displays the utensils for porch living.

When entertaining on the porch, the setting
becomes a part of the décor. With a backdrop
of a marsh, a garden or other natural interest,
entertaining on the porch allows these backdrops
to become enveloping elements, surrounding
your guests with enchanting ambiance.

LEFT Arched openings let the marsh and porch coexist,
with gentle breezes blowing in through the screened openings. The curves of the table mimic the arches.

RIGHT Treasures from land and sea, garden and gulf, make
for an elegant porch table setting. The hues of the hydran-
geas and shells meld into the greens of palmetto fronds.

Porches for Entertaining

Taking cues from the garden and nature is completely apropos for porch entertaining. Floral themes on linens, dinnerware and flatware continue the grace that bonds porch and home.

RIGHT A detail of classic Portmeirion tableware, this place setting evokes memories from yesteryear to yesterday.

Porches for Entertaining

A moment on the porch may set our solace for the day or provide the venue for after-dinner entertainment or a nightcap. Soothing palettes, comfortable surroundings and punches of color give porches charm.

ABOVE Accents abound to brighten our porches. The crisp whiteness of linen napkins bonds with the tortoiseshell flatware and tray. A hibiscus blossom punctuates this porch scene with vibrant color.

RIGHT A little corner of paradise captures the view and embraces the scene.

From within
the home's four
walls, this porch
extends into the
garden, nature and
light. Dining and
relaxing go hand
in hand, and festive
tableaus make this
vista ever more
pleasant.

Porches for Entertaining

LEFT A bounty of textures, colors, prints and flowers
weaves a tapestry of true delight and jovial porch living.

Porches for Entertaining

LEFT Divinely green glass plates harken the hues of the natural surroundings for this tablescape. The sun setting over and through the trees and over the sea casts ephemeral, fleeting light for this porch.

RIGHT A pitcher of lemonade and lush planters await enjoyment by those fortunate enough to sit a spell.

Porches for Entertaining

LEFT Prepped and ready. This porch is set for entertaining as a direct extension of the home into the garden.

ABOVE LEFT Zinnias snipped from the garden create a constellation of blossoms for the table's center. Vintage glass bottles boast their garden catches with crispness and clarity.

ABOVE RIGHT With a cacophony of complements— silver and rattan, ceramic and linen, bold lettering and soft flowers—the tableau as a whole highlights the best of porch entertaining.

Your party list may run for miles or be set at a few. Whatever the length of your guest list, a corner of the porch set elegantly is always de rigueur for entertaining, whether for seated dining or a refilling station for beverages and canapés. Displays grown on the porch may serve as centerpieces, connecting the garden and porch tableau.

Porches for Entertaining

LEFT Canopied by gracious oak limbs, this porch is now one with garden, for it boasts as many blossoms as the flower borders beyond.

Porches for Entertaining

Sans screens or glass, the open-air variety is a porch in its purest form. Groupings for dining, lounging and relaxing may fill the space, and, like the porch itself, may double in their usage. We might dine at a table or hold a plate on our lap in turn, relishing the ebb and flow of the indoors and outside while embracing porch living.

LEFT A chandelier donned with garden trappings adds whimsy to this garden-themed porch. Spaces for reclining and relaxing abound here with comfortable elegance.

ABOVE The porch as place for entertaining is highlighted with a table set for conversation and dining. The view onto the countryside is framed by sheers, softening the stonework and further playing on the sets of complements this porch offers.

111

Porches for Entertaining

LEFT Plates and other table setting accoutrements are balanced on one end of this porch table, primed for a lovely buffet dinner or ready for each guest to grab their own place setting for their choice porch seat.

RIGHT The graceful curves of live oak limbs are repeated in the arms of the chairs. Blues, golds and greens mark this luncheon theme, too, as mimics of nature abounding just beyond the porch door.

Porches for Entertaining

Grandest of porch settings can make for even the most intimate social gatherings. Lofty ceilings and open sides allow for marvelous ventilation too. A porch's architecture should encase the home and nature as one.

RIGHT Muted tones of earthy hues balance the veil of green just beyond the porch. Such a color scheme allows for zests of color to truly pop.

Doors opening from within the home onto a porch link the spaces. Porch shutters may serve as accompaniment to further the balance between landscape and living space. We yearn to be outside while comforted by inside charms, thus the appeal of porches.

Porches for Entertaining

LEFT Watermelon and wine—a summer sangria and a seasonal fruit pair together on this porch. Red, white and blue classically combine here as well.

Porches for Entertaining

Akin to a nest
within the trees,
we also construct
our porches from
nature's offerings.
Stone and timber,
reed and grass,
woven fibers and fired
clay—all can create
a porch "nest" for
our own enjoyment
and comfort.

RIGHT Punches of greens pop against this brown-on-brown palette, similar to the land, soil and bark beyond.

GARDEN PORCHES

The garden need not be limited to beds and borders, for the porch lends itself as an extraordinary host for planters and pots, herbs and flowers, plant collections and garden accessories. The garden porch is the midway point of home and garden proper, a destination central for those traversing between the two.

LEFT A snapshot of garden jewels. An assortment of plants is anchored by galvanized tin planters.

Garden Porches

Those that garden find their porches to be
more than vehicles leading into the home.
They are places of retreat, refuge and
rejuvenation, architectural outcrops to survey
the gardens beyond.

ABOVE A compilation of magazines to inspire and educate
the gardener is topped with a favorite pair of snips: a gardener
must be ready at all times to prune or pluck the perfect posie.

RIGHT The larger the porch the larger the planters. Gatherings
of smaller planers work to create a mass of flora too.

Garden Porches

ABOVE LEFT The blue-greens of the succulent foliage is carried further by the porch swing's hue.

ABOVE RIGHT Garden boots, pots of cabbage and a table for plant display are delightful trimmings for the entrance to this bucolic porch.

RIGHT A bright and cheery corner of a sun porch is perfect for growing plants. Jade, cabbages and a gorgeous begonia are happy as larks here in filtered sun.

Often the view
approaching the
porch can rival the
view *from* the porch.
Paths through
gardens leading
to screened, open
or glassed porches
make the journey
more joyous for those
passing toward these
destinations.

Garden Porches

LEFT The width of this sun porch is matched by a
patch of landscape, creating architectural balance
between home and garden.

LEFT Potted bromeliads, aspidistra, asparagus fern and palm all find a home on this porch set amidst garden and marsh.

ABOVE LEFT From garden porch to garden shed: the kitchen garden links the two appropriately enough.

ABOVE RIGHT Foliage souvenirs from a garden foray are elegantly displayed on a table on this garden porch.

When garden
space becomes
problematic, the
porch becomes a
panacea for plants,
spilling out of
planters, window
boxes and pots.
Such plantings are
a guest's luscious
first encounter
with our home's
persona.

LEFT Staggered on steps leading to the
porch, pots billowing with seasonal color
guide us onto the porch and into our home.

RIGHT A bench and planters—welcome
"mats" of sort on a side porch entrance to
this lovely home.

Garden Porches

ABOVE LEFT A cornucopia of fall's grandeur is collected and displayed on this porch's hearth-stone. Tonal greens, too, can celebrate the season.

ABOVE RIGHT A bouquet of vibrant green chry-santhemums and nandina berries accessorizes a porch table with garden flare.

RIGHT View into the garden from the rear porch. A concrete bench reiterates the craftsmanship of the handsome stonework wall and path.

Garden Porches

LEFT In urban settings, often the porch is the gardener's only outlet. A small tree adds big pizzazz to this garden porch.

ABOVE LEFT Red geraniums are hallmarks of porches, blooming out of their planters with cheerful zest. Lime green sweet potato vines enhance the blooms in the background.

ABOVE RIGHT Greens from the garden grace the porch. For height and a dose of drama—potted palmetto.

Garden Porches

Whether you have a pot or a plot, the porch also can be another gardening venue. Corners, tabletops and ledges all make for wonderful niches to extend your garden's square footage. The porch and garden become one with such planted additions.

ABOVE LEFT A pillow with a fern frond motif softens the corner of a porch swing, while a magnolia screens the porch, adding further shade and privacy.

ABOVE RIGHT A specimen begonia finds a happy home on this shady porch. With a grand garden just beyond the porch screen, this potted jewel is just a token of the whole setting.

RIGHT A bouncing board painted in traditional black/green, glasses of lemonade and a cache of potted specimens create an attractive scene on this garden porch.

From our porches
we descend into our
landscape and into
our gardens. Here
we will work and
play and enjoy the
nature surrounding
our homes but return
again to our porches,
piazzas, verandahs,
and loggias—the
cycle of porch living.

Garden Porches

LEFT Tennessee stack stone and Pennsylvania blue stone
match as tread and riser for these steps connecting porch,
pool and garden.

Garden Porches

LEFT A bright and sunny window ledge of a sun porch is just the place to display a prized begonia and a treasure from a trip taken years ago.

RIGHT Gardening on a porch requires sources of water. An antique watering can fits the bill and brings nourishing moisture to this collection of topiaries.

Manual of
Woody Landscape Plants

Manual of
Woody Landscape Plants   Michael A. Dirr

Garden Porches

LEFT Baskets bearing the fruit of our labors. The garden porch can host our bouquets, nosegays, arrangements and floral creations. This sideboard is set on the porch to bestow its guests with refreshments for taste and sight.

ABOVE LEFT More garden buds burst forth from a vase to create an homage to the season. When the garden is your floral resource, the possibilities are boundless.

ABOVE RIGHT Morning light gives these angel wing begonias the light they need. The earthen pots and palette are neutral enough to allow the greens of the backdrop and planters to give this corner of the garden some pop.